Looking After Animals

by Claire Llewellyn

We need to look after animals.

Animals need to eat.

We give food to the birds.

Animals need to drink.

We give water to the camels.

Animals need to sleep.

We give a bed to the donkeys.

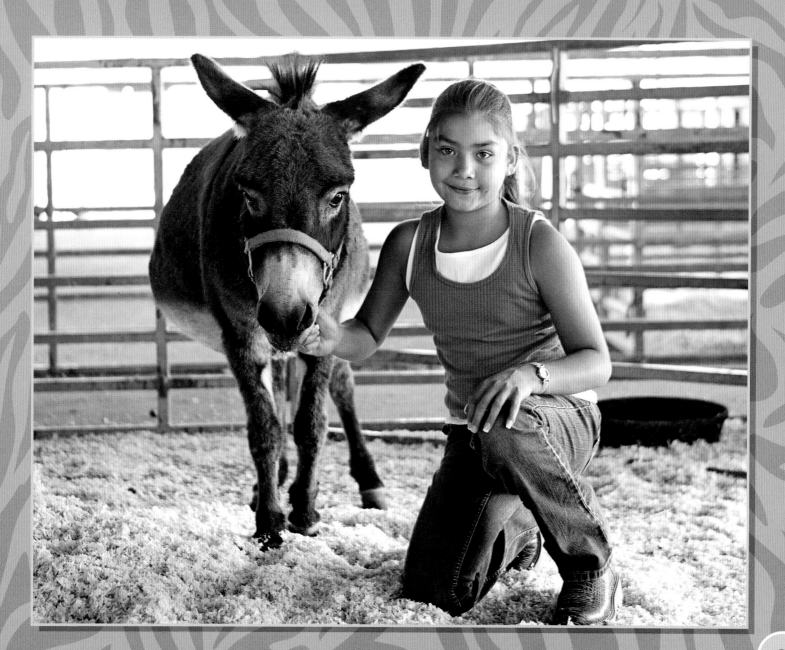

Animals need to play.

We give toys to the cats.

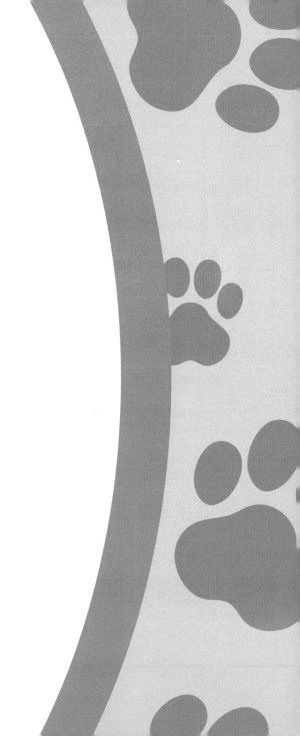

Animals need to wash.

We give a bath to the elephants.

We need to look after animals.

Looking after Animals Claire Llewellyn

Reading notes written by Sue Bodman and Glen Franklin

Using this book

Developing reading comprehension

The children in this book care for the animals, attending to their basic needs. A simple text with a repetitive structure and familiar content, the book has some features of an early non-chronological report through the inclusion of photographs and in referring to generic participants (*'cats'*, *'donkeys'*), rather than specific participants – 'this donkey', 'my cat', for example.

Grammar and sentence structure

- Three whole-sentence structures across the book each including at least one high frequency word.
- Simple punctuation (capital letters and full stops) occurs in the same position on each page.

Word meaning and spelling

- The changing nouns and verbs on each page are strongly supported by illustrations, and by recognition of the initial letter.
- A number of familiar high frequency words are included to aid development of fast, fluent reading, even at this early band.

Curriculum links

Science – Caring for school pets or creatures in the school wildlife garden would provide a good link with this book. The book could also support studies of different animal habitats – see 'Animal Homes' (Pink A band in the Cambridge Reading Adventures).

PSHE – A topic on people who help could include vets and others who care for animals.

Learning Outcomes

Children can:

- attend to print detail, including one-to-one matching across a line of text
- read some high-frequency words
- use phonic knowledge to work out some simple words.

A guided reading lesson

Book Introduction

Talk to the children about animals: *Do you keep animals at home? Who looks after them? Do you help?* Draw out that we need to do to look after animals.

Give a book to each child and read the title to them.

Orientation

Give a brief overview of the book, using the sentence structures from the text: *In this book, some children look after animals. They give the animals what they need to stay healthy, just like you do for your animals.*

Preparation

Page 2: Say: *I will read this page. I want you to track the words on the page in your own book as I read. Remember to point under each word, so that you can see them clearly.*

Pages 4 and 5: Discuss the picture, pointing out that the child is filling up a bird feeder. This is important to establish as there are